◆ Target 目標

　本ワークブックは、暗記に頼らず頭の中で考えながら、自分の言葉で英語を話せるようになることを目標に作られています。どのようにしてそれが可能になるのか？　それは動詞を Cue Word として利用することで可能になります。

　Cue とは、映画や舞台等での台詞の出だしとなる言葉のことをいいます。ではなぜ動詞なのか？　英語の文は、動詞を中心に組み立てられています。つまり動詞が決まれば、主語、目的語、補語等が、さらに形容詞や副詞などの修飾語も決まってくるのです。だから、動詞 Cue Word を見ただけで、英文が頭の中で組み立てられるという訳です。実に理に叶った学習法といえます。実際この学習法を利用した人たちから「考え、思い出しながら英語を話すことが出来た。」という感想が多く寄せられています。そして、暗記に頼らず考えながら英語を自分の言葉で話す力をつけることによって、英会話の応用力・汎用力の向上が期待できるわけです。

　また、このワークブックでの学習では、各 Unit のサンプル英文が、イントロダクション（導入）・ボディ（本論）・コンクルージョン（結論）を意識した構成になっています。学習者がこのサンプル英文を参考に英文を書いて、Cue words カードを作成し、このカードを見ながら英語を話すことによって、論理的に話す練習にもなります。

　これまでの学習で培った英語力をベースに、少しだけ目先を変えた本ワークブックで練習をすれば、英語が話せる自分を再発見することができるでしょう。英語を楽しく自信を持って話せる自分を想像してみませんか？

1. 動詞 cue word を見ただけで、英文が頭の中で組み立てられる

2. 考えながら、思い出しながら英語を話せる

3. 英会話の応用力・汎用力が期待できる

4. 論理的に話す練習になる

5. 英語を楽しく自信を持って自分の言葉で話せる

◆ How to Learn 学習の進め方

各 Unit を以下の手順で学習を進めることをおすすめします。

Step 1 　サンプル英文を読む 　＊英文の内容、文法、構成に注目
　　　　　↓
Step 2 　英文原稿を作成 　＊サンプル英文を参考に中学生レベルの英語で原稿作成
　　　　　↓
Step 3 　Cue Cards の作成 　＊原稿に書いた動詞を巻末 Cue Cards の下線に記入
　　　　　↓
Step 4 　音読練習 　＊英文原稿の音読練習
　　　　　↓
Step 5 　スピーチ 　＊切り取った Cue Cards を見ながらスピーチ

STEP1.

Unit のサンプルのスピーチ英文（U1-1）を読みます。この時に英文が、イントロダクション（導入）、ボディ（本論）1/2、コンクルージョン（結論） の構成であることを確認します。

SELF INTRODUCTION

Hello! My name is Mari. I would like to introduce myself. I'm a university student and majoring* in economics. I was born in 2007 in Matsumoto of Nagano prefecture in Japan. Now I'm living alone in Tokyo. I have two brothers. My older brother's name is Riku and my younger brother's name is Rui. They are living in Matsumoto with our parents. I am a very friendly and outgoing person. I like meeting new people, although I'm a little shy. Today, I will talk about my hobbies and my dream.

I like to listen to music. I especially like J-pop music. My favorite musician is Aimyon. The music and lyrics she writes are very exciting and touching. I think she is a genius. I also like to play tennis. I belong to the tennis club at my university, where about 20 students enjoy playing tennis almost every

---

day. We are all good friends and learn a lot of things from each other.

Now I have a dream to travel around the world. I want to meet a lot of people all over the world and learn various things, such as culture and ways of thinking. To make my dream come true, I have to study English. Studying English is not easy for me, but I don't want to give up on my dream. So, I would be glad if you all would study and speak English with me.

Thank you very much for listening. I look forward to meeting you again, and I hope we can all be friends. Do you have any questions?（264 words）

*major in 〜を専攻する

STEP 2.
サンプル英文を参考に、同じテーマで自分のスピーチ英文の原稿を Step 3 の用紙に書きます。この時に各構成の中がさらに入れ子のように構成されています。

（例 1）英文原稿の構成

Introduction ：　Salutation（挨拶）

Attention Getter（注意を引く）

Main Idea（本旨）

Overview（スピーチの概要）

Body 1 ：　本旨の説明

Body 2 ：　本旨の説明

Conclusion ：　Summary（要約）/ Final Comment（自分の意見）

Closing（結び）

STEP 3.

下の例を参考に英文スピーチの原稿を各自作成します。

（例）**Unit 1** No.　　Name:　　　　Date ／

"Hi! Nice to Meet You!"

《**Introduction**》 Salutation* & Attention Getter:	Hello, my name is Mari. I'm a university student and majoring in
Main Idea**:	economics. I'd like to introduce myself. Now I'm living in Tokyo.
Family:	I have two brothers. My older brother is Riku. My younger is Rui.
Personality:	I'm friendly and outgoing person. But I'm a little shy.
Overview***:	Today, I'll talk about my hobbies and my dream.
《**Body 1**》 My Hobbies:	I like listening to music. I especially like J-pop music. My favorite
	musician is Aimyon. The music she writes are exciting and touching.
	I also like to play tennis. I belong to the tennis club at my university,
	where 20 students enjoy playing tennis. We are good friends.
《**Body 2**》 My Dream:	Now I have a dream to travel around the world. I want to meet a lot of
	people all over the world and learn various things such as culture and
	ways of thinking. To make my dream come true, I have to study English.
	So, I'd be glad if you all study and speak English with me.
《**Conclusion**》 Summary:	Thank you very much for your listening. I look forward to meeting you
Closing:	again, and I hope we can all be friends. Do you have any questions?

*Salutation: 挨拶　**Main Idea: 本旨　***Over view: 外観

STEP 4.

Cue Cards を作りましょう。

◉キューカードの作り方

① 各自が作成した英文から動詞 cue words（一般動詞・Be 動詞）を拾って、Cue Card の下線上に記入します。

② 一般動詞には、それ自体にその主語や目的語、副詞などを想起させる情報が含まれているため、一般動詞の動詞 cue words を見れば、文章が頭の中で自動的に組み立てられます。

（例）　__play__

Be 動詞には、一般動詞のような情報はあまり含まれていないため、Cue Card には Be 動詞＋補語の組み合わせを記入します。

（例）　__am happy__

文が完結する目印として // を記します。

（例）　<u>am happy //</u>

③ 記入する下線が余ったときは、他の単語を記入してもかまいませんが、下線上には 1 単語のみ記入しましょう。

④ 記入が終わったら、キリトリセンで切り取り、この Cue Cards を見ながらスピーチをします。本文を暗記する必要はありません。準備は数回本文を音読するだけで十分です。

⑤ Cue Cards だけでスピーチをすることに不安を感じるかもしれませんが、上手に話す必要はありません。ゆっくりと思い出しながら話しましょう。心配する必要はありません。なぜなら、ゆっくりでも思い出しながら話すことこそ、自分の言葉で英語を話している証拠なのですから。

（例）**Unit 1** Re: Hi! Nice to Meet You!

Unit 1 **Hi! Nice to Meet You!**

no. 1 1 1 1 name Mari

date: / score: A ・ B ・ C

≪ **INTRODUCTION** ≫
Salutation & Attention Getter:

is Mari//　　'm a university//　　_____
Main Idea:

introduce//　'm living//　　study
Family:

is Riku//　　is Rui//　　_____
Personality:

'm friendly//　'm a little//　　_____
Overview:

Today　　talk//　　_____

Unit 1 **Hi! Nice to Meet You!**

≪ **BODY 2** ≫
Dream:

have　　to travel//　　want

to meet　　and learn//　　To make

have to speak//　study　　speak//

if　　study　　speak//

_____　_____　_____

キリトリセン

Unit 1 **Hi! Nice to Meet You!**

≪ **BODY 1** ≫
Hobbies:

like//　　Especially like　is Aimyon//

writes　　are exciting//　also like

to play//　　belong//　　enjoy//

are good friends//　　_____　_____

キリトリセン

Unit 1 **Hi! Nice to Meet You!**

≪ **CONCLUSION** ≫
Summary:

Thank//　　look//　　hope

be friends//　　_____　_____
Closing:

Do you have//　　_____　_____

_____　_____　_____

STEP 5.

英文原稿を見ながら音読練習をしましょう。

STEP 6.

キューカードを見ながらスピーチをします。聞き手は以下の PEER ASSESSMENT SHEET に聞き取った情報を記入します。

（例）　PEER-ASSESSMENT* SHEET

No._____ Name: _____

Presenter	Personality	Hobbies	Dream
1.　Mari	friendly, shy	listening music/shy	travel around the world
2.			
3.			
4.			
5.			
6.			
7.			
8.			
9.			
10.			
11.			
12.			
13.			
14			
15			
16			
17			
18			
19			
20			

*PEER ASSESSMENT: 相互評価

クラスの仲間たちに英語で自己紹介をしましょう。日本語よりも英語で自己紹介した方が気軽に自分のことを話せるかもしれません。また日本国内にいても、英語で自己紹介をする機会は実は多々あるものです。ただ慣れていないとなかなか話せませんね。後で、英語を勉強しておけばよかったなぁと後悔しないように、ゆっくりで構いませんので自分の言葉で英語で自己紹介しましょう。

この Unit では To 不定詞、動名詞の使い方も学びます。

Step 1. 次のサンプル英文を読んで自分のスピーチの参考にしましょう。

Hi! Nice to Meet You!

Hello! My name is Mari. I would like to introduce myself. I'm a university student and majoring* in economics. I was born in 2007 in Matsumoto of Nagano prefecture in Japan. Now I'm living alone in Tokyo. I have two brothers. My older brother's name is Riku and my younger brother's name is Rui. They are living in Matsumoto with our parents. I am a very friendly and outgoing person. I like meeting new people, although I'm a little shy. Today, I will talk about my hobbies and my dream.

I like to listen to music. I especially like J-pop music. My favorite musician is Aimyon. The music and lyrics she writes are very exciting and touching. I think she is a genius. I also like to play tennis. I belong to the tennis club at my university, where about 20 students enjoy playing tennis almost every day. We are all good friends and learn a lot of things from each other.

Now I have a dream to travel around the world. I want to meet a lot of people all over the world and learn various things, such as culture and ways of thinking. To make my dream come true, I have to study English. Studying English is not easy for me, but I don't want to give up on my dream. So, I would be glad if you all would study and speak English with me.

Thank you very much for listening. I look forward to meeting you again, and I hope we can all be friends. Do you have any questions?（264 words）

*major in 〜を専攻する

Step 2. 英文スピーチの原稿を作成します。

"Hi! Nice to Meet You!"

《**Introduction**》
Salutation &
Attention Getter:

Main Idea:

Family:

Personality:

Overview:

《**Body 1**》
My Hobbies:

《**Body 2**》
My Dream:

《**Conclusion**》
Summary:

Closing:

Step 3. 巻末の Cue Cards Unit1 に動詞を記入して完成させましょう。

Step 4. 音読練習をしましょう。

Step 5. Cue Cards を見ながらスピーチをします。
聞き手は PEER ASSESSMENT SHEET に内容を聞き取ります。

Unit 1 PEER-ASSESSMENT SHEET

No._____ Name:_____

Presenter	Personality	Hobbies	Dream
1.			
2.			
3.			
4.			
5.			
6.			
7.			
8.			
9.			
10.			
11.			
12.			
13.			

14.

15.

16.

17.

18.

19.

20.

21.

22.

23.

24.

25.

26.

27.

28.

29.

30.

故郷は身近過ぎて、知っているようで余り知らないことが沢山あります。故郷の良さを確認しながら、外国人に故郷を紹介することを想定して英語でスピーチをしましょう。英文を作成する際に、インターネットで故郷について調べてみても良いでしょう。故郷の英語版サイトにアクセスして英語の情報を入手すれば、英語の読解練習にもなるでしょう。

この Unit では、話の流れを導くシグナルワードの使い方も学びます。

Step 1. 次のサンプル英文を読んで自分のスピーチの参考にしましょう。

My Hometown

Hello, I'm Ken. I live in Kawasaki now. But I was born in Matsumoto of Nagano prefecture and grew up there. So, my hometown is Matsumoto. Today I will talk about some tourist spots in Matsumoto and what makes it special.

Matsumoto is located east of Nagano prefecture and is surrounded by the Chuu-bu Alps Mountains and the Northern Alps Mountains. About 200,000 people live there. Tourists who visit there are all captivated* by a lot of beautiful mountains and hot springs. Specifically, Kamikochi is a magnificent mountainous highland valley and designated* as one of Japan's National Cultural Assets. In spring, we enjoy cherry blossoms and many other flowers. In winter, we have snow and play winter sports such as skating, skiing and snowboarding.

Moreover, Matsumoto has various unique spots, such as the Ukiyoe Museum, the Kusama-Yayoi Museum, and the Forlkcraft Museum. In addition to these, every summer, the Saito Kinen Festival Matsumoto is held by Seiji Ozawa, his friends from abroad, and the citizens of Matsumoto. During the festival, a special concert and opera are held, and educational talks are given by the Saito Kinen Orchestra under the leadership of Seiji Ozawa.

I recommend you visit Matsumoto and enjoy the beautiful mountains, the unique museums and the music festival. Thank you for listening. （215 words）

*captivated 魅了される　*designated 選定されている

Step 2. 英文スピーチの原稿を作成します。

My Hometown:_____

《**Introduction**》
Salutation &
Attention Getter:

_____

Main Idea:

_____

_____

Overview:

_____

_____

《**Body 1**》
Tourist Spots:

_____

_____

_____

_____

_____

《**Body 2**》
Special Spots:

_____

_____

_____

_____

_____

《**Conclusion**》
Summary:

_____

Closing:

_____

_____

Step 3. 巻末の Cue Cards Unit 1 に動詞を記入して完成させましょう。

Step 4. 音読練習をしましょう。

Step 5. Cue Cards を見ながらスピーチをします。
聞き手は PEER ASSESSMENT SHEET に内容を聞き取ります。

Unit 2   PEER-ASSESSMENT SHEET

No._____ Name:_____

Presenter	Hometown	Tourist Spots	Unique Spots
1.			
2.			
3.			
4.			
5.			
6.			
7.			
8.			
9.			
10.			
11.			
12.			
13.			

14.

15.

16.

17.

18.

19.

20.

21.

22.

23.

24.

25.

26.

27.

28.

29.

30.

自分の宝物を紹介しながら、物の形や大きさを英語で説明しましょう。英語の数字を使って説明することに慣れていない人が多いようですが、その解決策は、英語の数字を実際に使ってみることです。そして、なぜそれが自分の宝物なのか理由を説明することで、説得力が増し相手に強く印象付けることができるでしょう。

Step 1. 次のサンプル英文を読んで自分のスピーチの参考にしましょう。

My Most Prized Possession: My Camera

　Hello, my name is Subaru. I have many possessions that I like. However, there is one that I cherish and care for more deeply than any other things. My most prized possession is my camera. It was a present from my parents. It's extremely useful and cool. In my speech, I will talk about the camera and then tell you why the camera is my prized possession.

　My camera is the newest model and was manufactured in Japan. It is blue, stylish and compact, and it has a lot of useful functions such as super auto-focus. I think the image quality of this camera is excellent. The camera is 7 cm tall, 10 cm wide, and 2 cm thick. The attached wrist strap is 10 cm in length. It weighs only 150g. I can always carry it in my pocket.

　The main reason why my camera is my favorite possession is because I can bring it almost anywhere I go. When I see a beautiful flower, mountain, or sky, I can take a beautiful picture of them easily. Furthermore, I can connect my camera to the Internet or my smartphone wherever I am. This is very important to me and useful, because I can store* the pictures in my computer immediately, edit* them and create my own world.

　Thanks to my camera, I can enjoy my life and broaden my world. That is why it is surely my most prized possession. Thank you for your listening. Do you have any questions? （251 words）

*store 保存する　*edit 編集する

My Most Prized Possession:_____

《**Introduction**》 Salutation & Attention Getter: Main Idea: Overview:	_____ _____ _____ _____ _____ _____
《**Body 1**》 Features: (color/dimensions/ quality/etc.)	_____ _____ _____ _____ _____ _____
《**Body 2**》 The Reasons:	_____ _____ _____ _____ _____ _____
《**Conclusion**》 Summary: Closing:	_____ _____ _____ _____

Step 3. 巻末の Cue Cards Unit3 に動詞を記入して完成させましょう。

Step 4. 音読練習をしましょう。

Step 5. Cue Cards を見ながらスピーチをします。
　　　　聞き手は PEER ASSESSMENT SHEET に内容を聞き取ります。

Unit 3　PEER-ASSESSMENT SHEET

No._____ Name:_____

Presenter	Possession	Features	Reasons
1.			
2.			
3.			
4.			
5.			
6.			
7.			
8.			
9.			
10.			
11.			
12.			
13.			

14.
_____ _____ _____

15.
_____ _____ _____

16.
_____ _____ _____

17.
_____ _____ _____

18.
_____ _____ _____

19.
_____ _____ _____

20.
_____ _____ _____

21.
_____ _____ _____

22.
_____ _____ _____

23.
_____ _____ _____

24.
_____ _____ _____

25.
_____ _____ _____

26.
_____ _____ _____

27.
_____ _____ _____

28.
_____ _____ _____

29.
_____ _____ _____

30.
_____ _____ _____

自分の夢を語るのは少し恥ずかしく思うかもしれません。でも英語で話すと、なぜか素直に言えるものです。言葉にすることで夢が目標になり、そして現実になるかもしれません。

この Unit では、現在完了形と未来形の使い方も学びます。

Step 1. 次のサンプル英文を読んで自分のスピーチの参考にしましょう。

My Dream Job: To Run My Own IT Company

Hello. My name is Steven Smith. Are you interested in information technology? I <u>have been</u> interested in computer science since I was a junior high school student. So, I'd like to get a job that has something to do with computers and information technology. Hopefully, I can run my own company one day. Firstly, I <u>will</u> talk about the business of computer and information technology. Secondly, I <u>will</u> present what to do in order to get a job in this industry.

Businesses related to computer and information technology are very exciting for me. Specifically, I am interested in designing and creating websites. More and more businesses and communications systems <u>will</u> depend on computer networks. However, computer network systems have to be secured* from computer viruses and hackers. I<u>'m going to</u> build an international website and offer a useful site that is safe for people around the world.

To make my dream come true, I want to learn about information technology and business, save money to establish my own IT company, and make friends who have the same dream as me. I have a lot of things to do, but the work to make my dream come true is exciting. Last but not least, I need to talk with a lot of people to deepen my understanding and widen my world view.

It may be a long time before I can achieve my dream, and it <u>will</u> not be easy. But I <u>will</u> never give up on my dream and will keep working hard. Thank you for listening. Do you have any questions? (264 words)

*secure 確保する

Step 2. 英文スピーチの原稿を作成します。

My Dream Job:＿＿＿＿＿＿＿＿＿＿

《**Introduction**》
Salutation &
Attention Getter:

Main Idea:

Overview:

《**Body 1**》
About the job:

《**Body 2**》
Preparation:
for the Job

《**Conclusion**》
Summary:

Closing:

Step 3. 巻末の Cue Cards Unit4 に動詞を記入して完成させましょう。

Step 4. 音読練習をしましょう。

Step 5. Cue Cards を見ながらスピーチをします。
聞き手は PEER ASSESSMENT SHEET に内容を聞き取ります。

Unit 4 PEER-ASSESSMENT SHEET

No._____ Name:_____

Presenter	About the Job	Preparation
1.		
2.		
3.		
4.		
5.		
6.		
7.		
8.		
9.		
10.		
11.		
12.		
13.		

14.

15.

16.

17.

18.

19.

20.

21.

22.

23.

24.

25.

26.

27.

28.

29.

30.

Unit 5
A Person from History That I Respect

あなたの尊敬する歴史上の人はだれですか？　明確に決まっていなくても、案外、心の どこかで意識しているものです。これを機会に自分の中で確認し、なぜその人が自分にとっ て尊敬の対象なのか考えてみましょう。あなた自身の再発見になるかもしれません。尊敬 する人をインターネットの英語版で検索すれば、英語の読解練習になるでしょう。

この Unit では、関係代名詞の使い方も学びます。

Step 1. 次のサンプル英文を読んで自分のスピーチの参考にしましょう。

A Person from History That I Respect:

Ryoma Sakamoto

Hello. My name is Ken Smith. Are you interested in history? I am very interested in Japanese history. Today, I will talk about Ryoma Sakamoto, <u>who</u> was a brave samurai in the Edo period of Japan. In my speech, firstly I will talk about his life and achievements. Then I will explain why I respect him.

Ryoma Sakamoto was born in Tosa, which is in Kochi prefecture of Japan about 200 years ago, at the end of the Edo period. When he was a child, Ryoma studied in a private school and learned Japanese fencing. Then he went to Edo to learn about foreign countries. The idea of the United States that "all men are created equal" inspired him to change Japan into a modernized country. He decided to dedicate his life to Japan. Eventually, he became the leaders of a movement to overthrow the Tokugawa Shogunate. Though he was assassinated at the age of 33, his achievements opened up Japan to the world.

The reason <u>why</u> I respect Ryoma is that he kept his dream that Japan would become a modernized country and that people would become happy and equal. Regardless of being a samurai, he worked as a merchant to make his dream come true. He dedicated his life to Japan. He was brave and free-spirited. I think that Ryoma is one of the greatest beacons* of hope for Japanese young people.

Ryoma worked for Japan at the cost of his life. He is still considered to be a real hero of Japan. We can learn a lot of things from him. Thank you for listening. Do you have any questions?（263words）　*beacon 指針となる人

Step 2. 英文スピーチの原稿を作成します。

A Person from History That I Respect:_____

《**Introduction**》
Salutation &
Attention Getter:

Main Idea:

Overview:

《**Body 1**》
Life &:
Achievement

《**Body 2**》
Reasons:

《**Conclusion**》
Summary:

Closing:

Step 3. 巻末の Cue Cards Unit5 に動詞を記入して完成させましょう。

Step 4. 音読練習をしましょう。

Step 5. Cue Cards を見ながらスピーチをします。
聞き手は PEER ASSESSMENT SHEET に内容を聞き取ります。

Unit 5 PEER-ASSESSMENT SHEET

No._____ Name:_____

Presenter	Person I Respect	Life & Achievement	Reasons
1.			
2.			
3.			
4.			
5.			
6.			
7.			
8.			
9.			
10.			
11.			
12.			
13.			

14.

15.

16.

17.

18.

19.

20.

21.

22.

23.

24.

25.

26.

27.

28.

29.

30.

世界にはたくさんの新発見がありますが、その中であなたが感銘を受けたものは何でしょうか？　仲間と共有して英語で話せたら楽しいですね。インターネットで英語版を調べてみると読解練習にもなります。

この Unit では、受動態の使い方も学びます。

Step 1. 次のサンプル英文を読んで自分のスピーチの参考にしましょう。

Exciting Discovery

Hello, I'm Miki. What discovery is exciting to you? For me, the great cave paintings of the Lascaux Cave in France are very exciting. I would like to talk about the paintings and tell you why I think they are so exciting.

The Lascaux Cave is located in southwestern France. It was accidentally discovered in 1940 by four teenagers. They were surprised to see nearly 2,000 figures of animals, humans and abstract signs in it. Most of the images were painted onto the walls using minerals and stones. The paintings are estimated to be 17,300 years old. After that, the Lascaux Cave was added to the list of UNESCO World Heritage Sites*.

In order to explain why I like the Lascaux Cave so much, I have to go back to my junior high school days. In a history lesson at school, I was very impressed by the picture of Lascaux in the text book. I couldn't believe that those beautiful, colorful pictures were 17,000 years old and painted by Cro-Magnon men in prehistoric times. I think the paintings are works of art and no less beautiful than modern arts.

The cave paintings of Lascaux are an exciting discovery in the world. Perhaps someday I will go to France to see the paintings. Thank you for listening. (216 words)

*UNESCO World Heritage Sites ユネスコ世界遺産

Step 2. 英文スピーチの原稿を作成します。

Exciting Discovery:_____

《**Introduction**》
Salutation &
Attention Getter: _____

Main Idea: _____

_____

Overview: _____

_____

《**Body 1**》
About the: _____
Discovery

_____

_____

_____

《**Body 2**》
Reasons: _____

_____

_____

_____

《**Conclusion**》
Summary: _____

Closing: _____

_____

Step 3. 巻末の Cue Cards Unit6 に動詞を記入して完成させましょう。

Step 4. 音読練習をしましょう。

Step 5. Cue Cards を見ながらスピーチをします。
聞き手は PEER ASSESSMENT SHEET に内容を聞き取ります。

Unit 6 PEER-ASSESSMENT SHEET

No._____ Name:_____

Presenter	Discovery	About Discovery	Reasons
1.			
2.			
3.			
4.			
5.			
6.			
7.			
8.			
9.			
10.			
11.			
12.			
13.			

14.

_____ _____ _____

15.

_____ _____ _____

16.

_____ _____ _____

17.

_____ _____ _____

18.

_____ _____ _____

19.

_____ _____ _____

20.

_____ _____ _____

21.

_____ _____ _____

22.

_____ _____ _____

23.

_____ _____ _____

24.

_____ _____ _____

25.

_____ _____ _____

26.

_____ _____ _____

27.

_____ _____ _____

28.

_____ _____ _____

29.

_____ _____ _____

30.

_____ _____ _____

If

「もしあなたが日本の首相だったら、何をしますか？」と仮定すると、あれもこれもと思い浮かぶかもしれません。特に 18 歳で選挙権を持つことができるようになって、より身近に感じられるテーマではないでしょうか？英語で自分の意見を述べることはハードルが高いかもしれませんが、海外の人から意見を求められることは多々あるようです。

この Unit では、仮定法の使い方も学びます。

Step 1. 次のサンプル英文を読んで自分のスピーチの参考にしましょう。

If I were the Prime-Minister of Japan

Hello. My name is Yuki. What <u>would you do, if you were </u>the Prime-Minister of Japan? Today I <u>would like</u> to give a speech on the theme of "<u>If I were</u> the Prime Minister of Japan." <u>If I were</u> the Prime Minister of Japan, I <u>would</u> work on environmental, fairness, and friendliness problems.

First, I <u>would</u> solve environmental problems. I <u>would</u> bring together scientific experts to work to find ways to slow down climate change. I <u>would</u> limit the production and use of single-use plastics. I <u>would</u> also clean up the world's oceans.

Second, I <u>would</u> ensure that all people in Japan are treated equally and fairly. Companies should be more regulated, stricter rules should be enforced, and fines should be imposed if necessary. For example, in Japan, it is difficult for women to return to work after giving birth because of the lack of affordable childcare. I <u>would</u> like to see more day-care centers and affordable* child-care for mothers.

Third, people think that Japan is friendly, but it is actually very closed. As Prime Minister, I <u>would</u> like to promote international events and make Japanese people aware of multiculturalism. Good relations with other countries also are very important. So, I <u>would</u> like to meet with the world's top leaders and build friendly relations.

Thank you very much for your kind attention. Today's speech made me realize that Japan has various problems to be solved. Do you have any questions? (240 words)

*affordable 手頃な

Step 2. 英文スピーチの原稿を作成します。

If I Were the Prime-Minister of Japan

《**Introduction**》
Salutation &
Attention Getter:

Main Idea:

Overview:

《**Body 1**》
First,:

《**Body 2**》
Second,:

《**Conclusion**》
Summary:

Closing:

Step 3. 巻末の Cue Cards Unit7 に動詞を記入して完成させましょう。

Step 4. 音読練習をしましょう。

Step 5. Cue Cards を見ながらスピーチをします。
聞き手は PEER ASSESSMENT SHEET に内容を聞き取ります。

Unit 7 PEER-ASSESSMENT SHEET

No._____ Name:_____

Presenter	First	Second
1.		
2.		
3.		
4.		
5.		
6.		
7.		
8.		
9.		
10.		
11.		
12.		
13.		

14.

_____ _____ _____

15.

_____ _____ _____

16.

_____ _____ _____

17.

_____ _____ _____

18.

_____ _____ _____

19.

_____ _____ _____

20.

_____ _____ _____

21.

_____ _____ _____

22.

_____ _____ _____

23.

_____ _____ _____

24.

_____ _____ _____

25.

_____ _____ _____

26.

_____ _____ _____

27.

_____ _____ _____

28.

_____ _____ _____

29.

_____ _____ _____

30.

_____ _____ _____

インターネットのおかげで、日本だけでなく世界中のニュースを瞬時にパソコンやスマホから知ることができます。とても便利な世の中になりました。そのニュースについて皆さんなりに感じること考えることがあると思います。それを海外の人たちと英語で話したいものですね。かなりハードルが高そうですが、言いたいことを英語に翻訳する必要はありません。コツは中学生レベルの英語で言いたいことを、前後、左右、斜めから説明すればよいのです。

　この Unit では、比較級、最上級の使い方も学びます。

Step 1. 次のサンプル英文を読んで自分のスピーチの参考にしましょう。

News & Opinion

　Hello, my name is Sam Wilson from America. Can you imagine living on just two U.S. dollars a day? Well, you may be surprised to hear it, but according to an article in a news magazine, about three billion people – half of the world's population – live on less than two dollars a day. It says this is because of the disparity* of wealth in the world. Today I'll briefly outline the article and then tell you how I feel and what I think about it.

　Surprisingly, the article says the three richest people in the world have more wealth than the 48 poorest countries in the world. It also said that one in two children live in poverty. It went on to say that 27,000 children die every day from extreme poverty. Furthermore, it looks at education, and said that one billion people are unable to read or sign their names but that 10 billion dollars would be enough to put every child into school.

　I was very shocked when I read the article. In this time of economic globalization, most people in poorer countries have much harder lives than before. On the other hand, a small number of rich people are expanding their wealth more and more. The same is true in Japan where the gap between the rich and the poor is growing. In my opinion, this global economic imbalance should be discussed a lot more and the disparity of wealth must be solved immediately.

　Thanks to this article, I learned about some problems related to globalization. In the future, I'd like to keep watching these problems. Thank you for your listening. I'll be glad to take your questions now.（281words）　*disparity 格差

Step 2. 英文スピーチの原稿を作成します。

News & Opinion

《**Introduction**》
Salutation &
Attention Getter:

Main Idea:

Personality:

Overview:

《**Body 1**》
About the News:

《**Body 2**》
My Opinion:

《**Conclusion**》
Summary:

Closing:

Step 3. 巻末の Cue Cards Unit8 に動詞を記入して完成させましょう。

Step 4. 音読練習をしましょう。

Step 5. Cue Cards を見ながらスピーチをします。
　　　　聞き手は PEER ASSESSMENT SHEET に内容を聞き取ります。

Unit 8　PEER-ASSESSMENT SHEET

No._____　Name:_____

	Presenter	About the News	Opinion
1.			
2.			
3.			
4.			
5.			
6.			
7.			
8.			
9.			
10.			
11.			
12.			
13.			

14. _____ _____ _____

15. _____ _____ _____

16. _____ _____ _____

17. _____ _____ _____

18. _____ _____ _____

19. _____ _____ _____

20. _____ _____ _____

21. _____ _____ _____

22. _____ _____ _____

23. _____ _____ _____

24. _____ _____ _____

25. _____ _____ _____

26. _____ _____ _____

27. _____ _____ _____

28. _____ _____ _____

29. _____ _____ _____

30. _____ _____ _____

no._____ name_____

date:_____/_____ score: A · B · C

≪ INTRODUCTION ≫

Salutation & Attention Getter:

_____ _____ _____

Main Idea:

_____ _____ _____

Family:

_____ _____ _____

Personality:

_____ _____ _____

Overview:

_____ _____ _____

キリトリセン

Unit 1 **Hi! Nice to Meet You!**

≪ BODY 2 ≫

Dream:

_____ _____ _____

_____ _____ _____

_____ _____ _____

_____ _____ _____

キリトリセン

キリトリセン

Unit 1 **Hi! Nice to Meet You!**

≪ BODY 1 ≫

Hobbies:

_____ _____ _____

_____ _____ _____

_____ _____ _____

_____ _____ _____

_____ _____ _____

キリトリセン

Unit 1 **Hi! Nice to Meet You!**

≪ CONCLUSION ≫

Summary:

_____ _____ _____

Closing:

_____ _____ _____

_____ _____ _____

Unit 2 My Hometown

no._____ name_____

date: _____/_____   score: A · B · C

≪ **INTRODUCTION** ≫

Salutation & Attention Getter:

_____ _____ _____

Main Idea:

_____ _____ _____

_____ _____ _____

Overview:

_____ _____ _____

キリトリセン

Unit 2 My Hometown

≪ **BODY 2** ≫

Unique Spots:

_____ _____ _____

_____ _____ _____

_____ _____ _____

_____ _____ _____

_____ _____ _____

キリトリセン

キリトリセン

Unit 2 My Hometown

≪ **BODY 1** ≫

Tourist Spots:

_____ _____ _____

_____ _____ _____

_____ _____ _____

_____ _____ _____

_____ _____ _____

キリトリセン

Unit 2 My Hometown

≪ **CONCLUSION** ≫

Summary:

_____ _____ _____

Closing:

_____ _____ _____

_____ _____ _____

no._____ name_____

date:_____/_____ score: A・B・C

≪ INTRODUCTION ≫

Salutation & Attention Getter:

_____ _____ _____

Main Idea:

_____ _____ _____

_____ _____ _____

_____ _____ _____

Overview:

_____ _____ _____

キリトリセン

≪ BODY 2 ≫

Reasons:

_____ _____ _____

_____ _____ _____

_____ _____ _____

_____ _____ _____

_____ _____ _____

キリトリセン

キリトリセン

≪ BODY 1 ≫

Features:

_____ _____ _____

_____ _____ _____

_____ _____ _____

_____ _____ _____

_____ _____ _____

キリトリセン

≪ CONCLUSION ≫

Summary:

_____ _____ _____

Closing:

_____ _____ _____

_____ _____ _____

Unit 4 My Dream Job

no.____ name_____

date: ____/____ score: A・B・C

≪ INTRODUCTION ≫

Salutation & Attention Getter:

_____ _____ _____

Main Idea:

_____ _____ _____

_____ _____ _____

_____ _____ _____

Overview:

_____ _____ _____

Unit 4 My Dream Job

≪ BODY 2 ≫

Preparation for the Job:

_____ _____ _____

_____ _____ _____

_____ _____ _____

_____ _____ _____

キリトリセン

キリトリセン

Unit 4 My Dream Job

≪ BODY 1 ≫

About the Job:

_____ _____ _____

_____ _____ _____

_____ _____ _____

_____ _____ _____

_____ _____ _____

キリトリセン

Unit 4 My Dream Job

≪ CONCLUSION ≫

Summary:

_____ _____ _____

_____ _____ _____

Closing:

_____ _____ _____

_____ _____ _____

Unit 5 A Person from History ...

no.____ name_____

date:_____ /_____ score: A · B · C

≪ INTRODUCTION ≫

Salutation & Attention Getter:

_____ _____ _____

Main Idea:

_____ _____ _____

_____ _____ _____

_____ _____ _____

Overview:

_____ _____ _____

キリトリセン

Unit 5 A Person from History ...

≪ BODY 2 ≫

Reasons:

_____ _____ _____

_____ _____ _____

_____ _____ _____

_____ _____ _____

_____ _____ _____

キリトリセン

Unit 5 A Person from History ...

≪ BODY 1 ≫

Life & Achievement:

_____ _____ _____

_____ _____ _____

_____ _____ _____

_____ _____ _____

_____ _____

Unit 5 A Person from History ...

≪ CONCLUSION ≫

Summary:

_____ _____ _____

_____ _____ _____

Closing:

_____ _____ _____

_____ _____ _____

キリトリセン

Unit 6 Exciting Discovery

no._____ name_____

date:_____ / _____ score: A · B · C

≪ **INTRODUCTION** ≫

Salutation & Attention Getter:

_____ _____ _____

Main Idea:

_____ _____ _____

_____ _____ _____

_____ _____ _____

Overview:

_____ _____ _____

Unit 6 Exciting Discovery

≪ **BODY 2** ≫

Reasons:

_____ _____ _____

_____ _____ _____

_____ _____ _____

_____ _____ _____

キリトリセン

Unit 6 Exciting Discovery

≪ **BODY 1** ≫

About the discovery:

_____ _____ _____

_____ _____ _____

_____ _____ _____

_____ _____ _____

_____ _____ _____

Unit 6 Exciting Discovery

≪ **CONCLUSION** ≫

Summary:

_____ _____ _____

_____ _____ _____

Closing:A

_____ _____ _____

_____ _____ _____

no._____ name_____

date:_____/_____ score: A · B · C

≪ **INTRODUCTION** ≫

Salutation & Attention Getter:

_____ _____ _____

Main Idea:

_____ _____ _____

Family:

_____ _____ _____

Personality:

_____ _____ _____

Overview:

_____ _____ _____

キリトリセン

≪ **BODY 2** ≫

_____ _____ _____

_____ _____ _____

_____ _____ _____

_____ _____ _____

キリトリセン

キリトリセン

≪ **BODY 1** ≫

_____ _____ _____

_____ _____ _____

_____ _____ _____

_____ _____ _____

_____ _____ _____

≪ **CONCLUSION** ≫

Summary:

_____ _____ _____

Closing:

_____ _____ _____

_____ _____ _____

キリトリセン

Unit 8 News & Opinion

no._____ name_____

date:_____ / _____ score: A · B · C

<u>≪ **INTRODUCTION** ≫</u>

Salutation & Attention Getter:

_____ _____ _____

Main Idea:

_____ _____ _____

_____ _____ _____

Overview:

_____ _____ _____

キリトリセン

Unit 8 News & Opinion

<u>≪ **BODY 2** ≫</u>

My Opinion:

_____ _____ _____

_____ _____ _____

_____ _____ _____

_____ _____ _____

キリトリセン

キリトリセン

Unit 8 News & Opinion

<u>≪ **BODY 1** ≫</u>

About the News:

_____ _____ _____

_____ _____ _____

_____ _____ _____

_____ _____ _____

キリトリセン

Unit 8 News & Opinion

<u>≪ **CONCLUSION** ≫</u>

Summary:

_____ _____ _____

Closing:

_____ _____ _____

_____ _____ _____